# SCHOOL CHAPLAINCY

*The Role and Responsibilities of a School Chaplain*

Dr. Maxwell Shimba

Shimba Publishing, LLC.

Printed in the United States of America

SHIMBA
PUBLISHING

# TABLE OF CONTENTS

# INTRODUCTION

The role of a school chaplain is both unique and essential in the educational environment. A school chaplain provides spiritual support, guidance, and care to students, staff, and the school community. This chapter will explore the multifaceted responsibilities of a school chaplain, emphasizing the importance of faith in education and the chaplain's role in guiding young individuals on their spiritual and moral journeys.

Understanding the Role of a School Chaplain

A school chaplain serves as a spiritual leader, counselor, and mentor within the educational setting. Unlike teachers who focus primarily on academic instruction, chaplains address the spiritual and emotional needs of students. This role requires a deep understanding of faith, a compassionate heart, and the ability to connect with individuals of diverse backgrounds and beliefs.

Key Responsibilities

1. Spiritual Guidance: Chaplains provide spiritual direction to students, helping them explore and deepen their faith. This includes organizing prayer sessions, leading religious services, and offering Bible studies or faith-based discussions.

2. Pastoral Care: Providing emotional support and counseling to students and staff is a crucial aspect of the chaplain's role. Chaplains are available to listen to personal concerns, offer guidance during difficult times, and provide comfort in times of grief or crisis.

3. Moral and Ethical Education: Chaplains contribute to the moral and ethical development of students by teaching values such as respect, integrity, compassion, and responsibility. They often integrate these lessons into various school activities and programs.

4. Community Building: Fostering a sense of community within the school is another important responsibility. Chaplains organize events and activities that promote inclusivity, unity, and mutual respect among students and staff.

5. Interfaith Dialogue: In increasingly diverse educational environments, chaplains must navigate interfaith dynamics with sensitivity and respect. They facilitate discussions that promote understanding and acceptance of different religious beliefs and practices.

The Importance of Faith in Education

Faith plays a significant role in the holistic development of young individuals. Integrating faith into education helps students develop a strong moral foundation, resilience, and a sense of purpose. It also encourages students to reflect on their values and beliefs, fostering personal growth and self-awareness.

Benefits of Faith-Based Education

1. Moral Compass: Faith-based education provides students with a clear moral compass, guiding their decisions and actions. This foundation helps them navigate the complexities of life with integrity and ethical awareness.

2. Emotional Resilience: Spiritual practices, such as prayer and meditation, offer students tools to manage stress, anxiety, and other emotional challenges. Faith can be a source of strength and comfort, particularly during difficult times.

3. Sense of Purpose: Understanding and embracing one's faith can give students a sense of purpose and direction. It helps them set meaningful goals and strive towards a life that aligns with their values and beliefs.

4. Community and Belonging: Faith-based education fosters a sense of community and belonging. Students who share common beliefs and values often form strong,

supportive relationships that enhance their educational experience.

Guiding the Young: Practical Strategies for Chaplains

Effective school chaplaincy requires a combination of empathy, active listening, and practical strategies. Here are some key approaches chaplains can use to guide young individuals in their faith journey:

Building Trust and Rapport

1. Active Listening: Truly listen to students' concerns and experiences without judgment. Show empathy and understanding, creating a safe space for them to express themselves.

2. Being Present: Make an effort to be visibly present and accessible within the school. Attend school events, visit classrooms, and engage with students during breaks and lunchtime.

3. Confidentiality: Maintain confidentiality in all interactions, ensuring that students feel safe sharing their personal and spiritual struggles.

Encouraging Spiritual Practices

1. Prayer and Meditation: Encourage students to develop regular prayer or meditation practices. Provide guidance on different methods and create opportunities for communal prayer.

2. Scripture Study: Organize Bible study groups or faith-based reading sessions. Help students explore and understand religious texts, encouraging them to apply these teachings to their lives.

3. Service Projects: Involve students in community service projects that align with their faith values. This not only strengthens their faith but also teaches them the importance of compassion and service to others.

Promoting Inclusivity and Respect

1. Interfaith Activities: Organize events and discussions that promote interfaith understanding and respect. Encourage students to learn about and appreciate different religious traditions.

2. Conflict Resolution: Mediate conflicts that arise from religious or cultural differences. Teach students conflict resolution skills based on mutual respect and understanding.

3. Inclusive Practices: Ensure that all school activities and programs are inclusive and respectful of diverse religious beliefs. Advocate for policies that support religious freedom and expression.

Case Studies: Successful School Chaplaincy Programs

To illustrate the impact of effective school chaplaincy, let's examine a few case studies:

Case Study 1: Building Community through Service

At a large urban high school, the chaplain initiated a series of community service projects, including volunteering at local shelters, organizing food drives, and participating in environmental clean-up efforts. These projects not only provided practical help to the community but also fostered a sense of unity and purpose among students. Many students reported feeling more connected to their peers and more committed to their faith as a result of these activities.

Case Study 2: Supporting Students in Crisis

In a rural school, the chaplain played a critical role in supporting students during a period of crisis. Following a tragic accident that claimed the life of a beloved teacher, the chaplain organized grief counseling sessions, provided one-on-one support to grieving students, and held memorial services to honor the teacher's memory. The chaplain's presence and support helped students navigate their grief and find comfort in their faith.

Conclusion

The role of a school chaplain is integral to the spiritual and moral development of students. By providing spiritual guidance, pastoral care, and promoting inclusivity, chaplains play a crucial role in shaping the character and faith of young individuals. Through their dedicated efforts, chaplains help create a nurturing and supportive educational environment where students can thrive both academically and spiritually.

School Chaplain

xi

DR. MAXWELL SHIMBA

CHAPTER 01

---

## UNDERSTANDING THE ROLE OF A SCHOOL CHAPLAIN

A school chaplain serves as a spiritual leader, counselor, and mentor within the educational setting. Unlike teachers who focus primarily on academic instruction, chaplains address the spiritual and emotional needs of students. This role requires a deep understanding of faith, a compassionate heart, and the ability to connect with individuals of diverse backgrounds and beliefs.

Spiritual Leadership

As spiritual leaders, school chaplains are responsible for nurturing the faith lives of students, staff, and the broader school community. This involves organizing and leading prayer sessions, religious services, and spiritual retreats. Chaplains create an environment where students can explore and deepen their faith, ask questions, and engage in meaningful discussions about spirituality and ethics. They provide resources for spiritual growth, such as devotional materials and opportunities for service projects that align with the school's values.

Counseling and Emotional Support

One of the core responsibilities of a school chaplain is to offer counseling and emotional support to students and staff. This involves being a trusted confidant and advisor, someone students can turn to during times of personal crisis or emotional distress. Chaplains provide a safe and confidential space for individuals to share their struggles, whether they are dealing with grief, anxiety, relationship issues, or other personal challenges. Through active listening and empathetic support, chaplains help individuals find hope and healing.

Mentoring and Guidance

Chaplains play a crucial mentoring role, guiding students in their personal and spiritual development. This includes helping students develop a strong moral compass and ethical framework based on their faith values. Chaplains encourage students to reflect on their actions, make responsible decisions, and develop character traits such as integrity, compassion, and respect for others. They also offer guidance on navigating the complexities of adolescence, providing wisdom and support as students face academic pressures, social dynamics, and future planning.

Building Community

A significant aspect of a school chaplain's role is fostering a sense of community within the school. Chaplains work to create an inclusive and welcoming environment where all students feel valued and supported. This involves organizing community-building activities, such as interfaith dialogues, cultural celebrations, and service projects that bring students together and promote understanding and unity. By encouraging students to appreciate and respect diversity, chaplains help build a cohesive and harmonious school community.

Interfaith Engagement

In today's diverse educational settings, chaplains must be adept at navigating interfaith dynamics. They facilitate interfaith engagement by organizing events and discussions that promote understanding and respect for different religious traditions. Chaplains help students learn about and appreciate the beliefs and practices of their peers, fostering an environment of mutual respect and inclusivity. This interfaith work is essential for preparing students to thrive in a multicultural and multi-religious world.

Advocacy and Policy Influence

Chaplains often play a role in advocating for the spiritual and emotional well-being of students within the school's administration. They work to ensure that school policies are inclusive and supportive of all students' religious and spiritual needs. This may involve advocating for spaces where students can pray or meditate, ensuring that religious holidays are respected, and promoting policies that support the mental health and well-being of the school community.

Conclusion

The role of a school chaplain is multifaceted and essential in nurturing the spiritual, emotional, and moral development of students. By serving as spiritual leaders, counselors, mentors, and community builders, chaplains help create a supportive and inclusive educational environment. Their work is vital in guiding young individuals on their spiritual journeys and helping them develop into compassionate, ethical, and resilient individuals.

## Spiritual Guidance

One of the primary responsibilities of a school chaplain is to provide spiritual guidance to students. This involves helping students explore and deepen their faith, and fostering an environment where spiritual growth is encouraged and supported. The chaplain's role in spiritual guidance includes several key activities:

Organizing Prayer Sessions

Prayer sessions are a fundamental aspect of spiritual guidance. Chaplains organize regular prayer sessions, creating opportunities for students to engage in communal prayer. These sessions can be held daily, weekly, or during special occasions, and they serve as a time for students to come together, reflect, and seek spiritual connection. Prayer sessions can take various forms, such as traditional prayers, meditative practices, or spontaneous prayers led by the chaplain or students.

Leading Religious Services

Chaplains also lead religious services, which are essential for the spiritual life of the school community. These services may include regular worship services, special ceremonies, and observances of religious holidays. By leading these services, chaplains provide a structured and meaningful way for students to practice their faith, participate in communal worship, and experience the rituals and traditions of their religion. Religious services offer a sense of belonging and community, reinforcing the spiritual foundation of the school.

Offering Bible Studies and Faith-Based Discussions

Another crucial aspect of spiritual guidance is offering Bible studies and faith-based discussions. Chaplains organize and lead Bible study groups where students can delve into scripture, discuss its meanings, and apply its teachings to their lives. These sessions provide a deeper understanding of religious texts and encourage critical thinking about faith. Additionally, chaplains facilitate faith-based discussions on various topics, such as ethical dilemmas, moral questions, and contemporary issues viewed through a spiritual lens. These discussions help students articulate their beliefs, challenge their perspectives, and grow in their faith.

Encouraging Personal Spiritual Practices

Beyond organized activities, chaplains encourage students to develop personal spiritual practices. This includes fostering habits such as daily prayer, meditation, and personal reflection. Chaplains provide resources and guidance on how to incorporate these practices into students' daily lives, helping them build a personal relationship with their faith.

Creating a Supportive Environment

Chaplains work to create a supportive environment where students feel comfortable exploring their spirituality. This involves being approachable and available for one-on-one spiritual counseling, offering a listening ear and personalized guidance. By building trust and rapport with students, chaplains ensure that they feel supported in their spiritual journeys.

Facilitating Interfaith Understanding

In schools with diverse religious populations, chaplains play a vital role in facilitating interfaith understanding. They organize interfaith events and discussions, helping students learn about different religious traditions and promoting respect and appreciation for diverse beliefs. This not only enriches students' spiritual lives but also fosters a culture of inclusivity and mutual respect within the school community.

Conclusion

Providing spiritual guidance is a central responsibility of a school chaplain. Through organizing prayer sessions, leading religious services, and offering Bible studies and faith-based discussions, chaplains help students explore and deepen their faith. By encouraging personal spiritual practices and creating a supportive environment, chaplains ensure that students feel valued and guided in their spiritual journeys. In facilitating interfaith understanding, chaplains contribute to a harmonious and inclusive school community, enriching the spiritual lives of all students.

**Pastoral Care**

Providing emotional support and counseling to students and staff is a crucial aspect of the chaplain's role. Pastoral care is about being present for the school community in times of need, offering a compassionate and listening ear, and providing guidance and comfort during challenging times. This dimension of a chaplain's responsibilities encompasses several key activities:

Listening to Personal Concerns

A fundamental part of pastoral care is being available to listen to the personal concerns of students and staff. Chaplains create a safe and confidential environment where individuals can express their thoughts and feelings without fear of judgment. By actively listening and showing empathy, chaplains help individuals feel heard and understood, which can be incredibly healing and validating.

Offering Guidance During Difficult Times

Life can be full of challenges, and students and staff often face difficult situations that require guidance and support. Whether it's academic stress, relationship issues, family problems, or personal struggles, chaplains provide a steady and compassionate presence. They offer practical advice, spiritual counsel, and emotional support, helping individuals navigate their difficulties with resilience and hope.

Providing Comfort in Times of Grief or Crisis

During times of grief or crisis, the role of a chaplain becomes even more vital. Whether dealing with the loss of a loved one, a traumatic event, or a school-wide tragedy, chaplains provide much-needed comfort and support. They offer a shoulder to cry on, a comforting word, and a reassuring presence. Chaplains may also organize and lead memorial services, prayer vigils, or other ceremonies that allow the school community to come together, mourn, and find solace.

Building Trust and Rapport

For pastoral care to be effective, chaplains must build trust and rapport with students and staff. This involves being approachable, consistent, and genuinely caring. Chaplains often engage with the school community through informal interactions, attending school events, visiting classrooms, and being present in common areas. By being a visible and trusted figure, chaplains create an environment where individuals feel comfortable seeking their support.

Providing One-on-One Counseling

Chaplains often provide one-on-one counseling sessions for students and staff. These sessions are tailored to the individual's needs, offering personalized support and guidance. Chaplains use various counseling techniques, grounded in empathy and active listening, to help individuals explore their emotions, identify coping strategies, and find a path forward. These sessions can be short-term, addressing immediate concerns, or long-term, supporting ongoing personal growth and healing.

Facilitating Support Groups

In addition to individual counseling, chaplains may facilitate support groups for students and staff who are dealing with similar issues. These groups provide a sense of community and shared understanding, allowing participants to support one another and gain strength from shared experiences. Topics for support groups can range from grief and loss to stress management, mental health, and more. Chaplains create a safe and supportive space for these groups, fostering a sense of belonging and mutual support.

Crisis Intervention

In times of crisis, chaplains are often at the forefront of the school's response efforts. They provide immediate emotional support and practical assistance, helping individuals and the community cope with the aftermath of the crisis. This may involve coordinating with other support services, offering spiritual guidance, and ensuring that those affected receive the help they need. Chaplains play a critical role in stabilizing the situation and helping the school community begin the healing process.

Promoting Well-Being

Beyond responding to crises and individual needs, chaplains also promote overall well-being within the school community. They organize workshops, seminars, and activities focused on mental health, emotional resilience, and spiritual well-being. By proactively addressing these areas, chaplains help create a healthier and more supportive school environment where students and staff can thrive.

Conclusion

Pastoral care is a cornerstone of a school chaplain's role. Through listening to personal concerns, offering guidance during difficult times, and providing comfort in times of grief or crisis, chaplains offer essential emotional and spiritual support to the school community. By building trust and rapport, providing one-on-one counseling, facilitating support groups, intervening in crises, and promoting overall well-being, chaplains create a nurturing and supportive environment where students and staff feel valued and cared for. Their presence and support help individuals navigate life's challenges with resilience and hope, contributing to a positive and compassionate school community.

## Moral and Ethical Education

Chaplains play a crucial role in the moral and ethical development of students, imparting values that are essential for their personal growth and for creating a positive school environment. This responsibility involves teaching and modeling values such as respect, integrity, compassion, and responsibility, and integrating these lessons into various school activities and programs.

Teaching Core Values

Chaplains actively teach core values that form the foundation of ethical behavior and moral decision-making. These values include:

1. Respect: Encouraging students to treat others with dignity and consideration, recognizing the inherent worth of every individual.

2. Integrity: Promoting honesty, transparency, and consistency in actions and words.

3. Compassion: Fostering empathy and kindness towards others, especially those in need or distress.

4. Responsibility: Instilling a sense of accountability for one's actions and the impact they have on others and the community.

Integrating Values into Curriculum and Activities

Chaplains integrate these core values into the broader curriculum and school activities. This may involve:

1. Classroom Discussions: Leading discussions on ethical dilemmas and moral questions, encouraging students

to think critically about their values and how they apply them in various situations.

2. Workshops and Seminars: Organizing workshops and seminars on topics such as ethics, character development, and social justice.

3. Service Projects: Coordinating community service projects that allow students to practice compassion and responsibility in real-world settings.

4. School Assemblies: Delivering talks and presentations during school assemblies that highlight important moral and ethical themes.

Role Modeling and Mentorship

Chaplains serve as role models for students, demonstrating the values they teach through their own behavior and interactions. By embodying respect, integrity, compassion, and responsibility, chaplains provide a living example for students to emulate. Additionally, chaplains offer mentorship, guiding students in their personal development and helping them navigate ethical challenges.

Creating a Values-Based Culture

Chaplains work to create a school culture that is grounded in strong moral and ethical values. This involves:

1. Policy Advocacy: Advocating for school policies that reflect and uphold core values, ensuring that the school environment is supportive and respectful for all.

2. Recognition Programs: Implementing programs that recognize and reward students for demonstrating exemplary moral and ethical behavior.

3. Conflict Resolution: Mediating conflicts and promoting peaceful and respectful resolution of disagreements, teaching students the importance of empathy and understanding.

Encouraging Self-Reflection

Part of moral and ethical education involves encouraging students to engage in self-reflection. Chaplains guide students in reflecting on their actions, understanding the consequences of their behavior, and considering how their choices align with their values. This reflective practice helps students develop a strong sense of self-awareness and moral responsibility.

Collaborative Efforts

Chaplains often collaborate with teachers, administrators, and parents to reinforce moral and ethical education. This collaborative approach ensures that the values being taught are consistently supported across different aspects of students' lives, creating a cohesive and unified message about the importance of ethical behavior.

Addressing Contemporary Issues

Chaplains also address contemporary ethical issues that students may encounter, such as cyberbullying, social media ethics, and environmental responsibility. By discussing these topics, chaplains help students understand how to apply their values in modern contexts and make ethical decisions in a complex and changing world.

Conclusion

Moral and ethical education is a key responsibility of school chaplains. Through teaching core values, integrating them into school activities, modeling ethical behavior, and fostering a values-based culture, chaplains contribute significantly to the personal and moral development of students. By encouraging self-reflection and addressing contemporary issues, chaplains equip students with the tools they need to navigate their lives with integrity, compassion, and responsibility. Their efforts help create a school environment where ethical behavior is the norm, and every individual is respected and valued.

## Community Building

Fostering a sense of community within the school is another important responsibility of a school chaplain. By organizing events and activities that promote inclusivity, unity, and mutual respect, chaplains help create a supportive and cohesive school environment where every individual feels valued and connected. This section will explore various strategies and initiatives that chaplains can implement to build a strong and inclusive school community.

Promoting Inclusivity

Inclusivity is a cornerstone of community building. Chaplains work to ensure that all students and staff feel welcomed and respected, regardless of their background, beliefs, or personal circumstances. This involves:

1. Celebrating Diversity: Organizing events that celebrate the diverse cultures, traditions, and backgrounds within the school community. These events can include cultural fairs, heritage days, and multicultural festivals.

2. Interfaith Dialogues: Facilitating interfaith dialogues and discussions that promote understanding and respect for different religious beliefs and practices. This helps to create an environment where everyone's faith is acknowledged and respected.

3. Inclusive Practices: Advocating for inclusive practices in school policies and programs, ensuring that all students have equal access to opportunities and resources.

Building Unity

Unity within the school community is essential for fostering a sense of belonging and collaboration. Chaplains play a key role in building unity through various initiatives:

1. Team-Building Activities: Organizing team-building activities and retreats that encourage students and staff to work together, build relationships, and develop a sense of camaraderie.

2. School-Wide Projects: Coordinating school-wide projects that bring the entire school community together to achieve a common goal, such as community service initiatives, environmental campaigns, or charity drives.

3. Shared Experiences: Creating opportunities for shared experiences, such as school assemblies, celebrations, and special events that reinforce a sense of collective identity and purpose.

Encouraging Mutual Respect

Mutual respect is fundamental to a healthy and positive school community. Chaplains encourage mutual respect through:

1. Respectful Communication: Teaching and modeling respectful communication, emphasizing the importance of listening, empathy, and understanding in interactions with others.

2. Conflict Resolution: Providing tools and training for conflict resolution, helping students and staff to navigate disagreements in a constructive and respectful manner.

3. Role Modeling: Serving as role models for respectful behavior, demonstrating through their actions how to treat others with kindness and consideration.

Organizing Community Events

Community events are a powerful way to bring people together and strengthen the bonds within the school. Chaplains can organize a variety of events that promote community spirit and engagement:

1. Social Events: Hosting social events such as picnics, dances, and family days that provide opportunities for informal interaction and relationship-building.

2. Service Projects: Coordinating service projects that involve the entire school community, fostering a sense of shared purpose and collective effort in making a positive impact.

3. Celebrations and Ceremonies: Planning and leading celebrations and ceremonies that mark important milestones, achievements, and transitions within the school community.

Creating Support Networks

Building a sense of community also involves creating support networks where individuals can find help and encouragement. Chaplains facilitate these networks by:

1. Peer Support Groups: Establishing peer support groups where students can connect with others who share similar experiences or challenges.

2. Mentorship Programs: Develop mentorship programs that pair students with older peers, staff, or community members who can provide guidance and support.

3. Resource Sharing: Coordinating the sharing of resources and information about available support services, ensuring that everyone in the community knows where to turn for help.

Conclusion

Community building is a vital responsibility of school chaplains. By promoting inclusivity, building unity, encouraging mutual respect, organizing community events, and creating support networks, chaplains help to create a vibrant and cohesive school environment. Their efforts ensure that every member of the school community feels valued, supported, and connected, contributing to a positive and nurturing educational experience for all. Through these initiatives, chaplains foster a sense of belonging and collaboration that enhances the overall well-being and success of the school community.

Interfaith Dialogue

In increasingly diverse educational environments, chaplains must navigate interfaith dynamics with sensitivity and respect. They play a crucial role in facilitating discussions that promote understanding and acceptance of different religious beliefs and practices. By fostering an atmosphere of respect and inclusivity, chaplains help create a harmonious school environment where all students feel valued and understood.

Understanding Interfaith Dialogue

Interfaith dialogue involves open and respectful communication between individuals of different religious traditions. The goal is not to change anyone's beliefs but to foster mutual understanding, respect, and cooperation. In a school setting, interfaith dialogue can help break down stereotypes, reduce prejudice, and build a community that values diversity.

Key Activities in Interfaith Dialogue

1. Organizing Interfaith Events

- Panel Discussions: Hosting panel discussions with representatives from different faith traditions to share their beliefs and practices. This provides students with a firsthand understanding of various religions.

- Interfaith Forums: Creating forums where students can engage in dialogue about their faith experiences and ask questions in a respectful and supportive environment.

- Cultural Celebrations: Organizing events that celebrate the religious and cultural diversity within the school. These events can include festivals, food fairs, and cultural performances that highlight different traditions.

2. Educational Programs

- Workshops and Seminars: Conducting workshops and seminars that educate students about different religions. Topics can include the history, beliefs, rituals, and ethical teachings of various faiths.

- Classroom Integration: Working with teachers to integrate interfaith education into the curriculum. This can involve guest speakers, field trips to places of worship, and the inclusion of religious texts in literature studies.

3. Promoting Respectful Communication

- Dialogue Skills Training: Providing students with training in dialogue skills, including active listening, empathy, and respectful questioning. These skills are essential for meaningful interfaith interactions.

- Conflict Resolution: Teaching students how to resolve conflicts that may arise from religious misunderstandings or differences. This includes strategies for finding common ground and maintaining respectful communication.

4. Creating Safe Spaces

- Safe Spaces for Discussion: Establishing safe spaces within the school where students can discuss religious topics without fear of judgment or hostility. These spaces encourage honest and open dialogue.

- Support Groups: Forming support groups for students who may feel marginalized or misunderstood because of their religious beliefs. These groups provide a sense of community and solidarity.

Benefits of Interfaith Dialogue

Interfaith dialogue offers numerous benefits to the school community:

1. Increased Understanding: Students gain a deeper understanding of different religious traditions, which reduces ignorance and promotes empathy.

2. Reduced Prejudice: Exposure to diverse beliefs helps break down stereotypes and prejudices, fostering a more inclusive environment.

3. Enhanced Critical Thinking: Engaging with different perspectives enhances students' critical thinking skills and their ability to analyze complex issues.

4. Stronger Community Bonds: Interfaith activities build stronger bonds within the school community, promoting unity and cooperation.

Challenges and Solutions

While interfaith dialogue is beneficial, it can also present challenges:

1. Resistance to Participation: Some students or staff may be reluctant to participate in interfaith activities. Chaplains can address this by emphasizing the importance of respect and understanding and by creating engaging and inclusive programs.

2. Misunderstandings: Misunderstandings or conflicts may arise during interfaith discussions. Chaplains should be prepared to mediate and provide guidance on respectful communication and conflict resolution.

3. Balancing Perspectives: Ensuring that all religious perspectives are represented and respected can be challenging. Chaplains should strive for inclusivity and balance in all interfaith activities.

Conclusion

Interfaith dialogue is a vital responsibility of school chaplains in today's diverse educational environments. By facilitating discussions that promote understanding and acceptance of different religious beliefs and practices, chaplains help create a respectful and inclusive school community. Through organizing interfaith events, promoting respectful communication, and creating safe spaces, chaplains foster an environment where all students feel valued and understood. The benefits of interfaith dialogue extend beyond the school, preparing students to navigate a diverse and interconnected world with empathy and respect.

CHAPTER 02

---

## IMPORTANCE OF FAITH IN EDUCATION

Faith plays a significant role in the holistic development of young individuals. Integrating faith into education helps students develop a strong moral foundation, resilience, and a sense of purpose. It also encourages students to reflect on their values and beliefs, fostering personal growth and self-awareness. This chapter will explore the various ways in which faith contributes to the educational experience and the overall development of students.

Developing a Strong Moral Foundation

Faith-based education provides students with a clear set of moral and ethical guidelines. These principles help shape their character and guide their actions both within and outside the school environment.

Teaching Core Values

Faith-based education emphasizes core values such as honesty, integrity, respect, and compassion. These values are often derived from religious teachings and are reinforced through daily practices and interactions. By learning and internalizing these values, students develop a strong moral compass that guides their behavior and decision-making processes.

Role Modeling

Teachers and chaplains in faith-based schools serve as role models for students, demonstrating how to live out these values in everyday life. Through their actions and interactions, they provide tangible examples of ethical behavior and integrity, inspiring students to follow suit.

Building Resilience

Faith can be a source of strength and resilience for students, helping them navigate the challenges and pressures of adolescence and academic life.

Coping Mechanisms

Faith-based education often includes teachings on how to cope with stress, anxiety, and other emotional challenges. Practices such as prayer, meditation, and reflection provide students with tools to manage their emotions and maintain a sense of inner peace during difficult times.

Community Support

Faith-based schools often foster a strong sense of community, where students feel supported and cared for by their peers and teachers. This network of support helps students build resilience and provides a safety net during times of crisis or personal struggle.

Fostering a Sense of Purpose

Understanding and embracing one's faith can give students a sense of purpose and direction. This sense of purpose is crucial for motivating students and helping them set and achieve meaningful goals.

Spiritual Growth

Faith-based education encourages students to explore their spirituality and deepen their relationship with their faith. This spiritual growth helps students find meaning and purpose in their lives, guiding their aspirations and efforts.

Service and Compassion

Many faith-based schools emphasize the importance of service and compassion towards others. By engaging in community service projects and acts of kindness, students learn the value of contributing to the well-being of others, further reinforcing their sense of purpose and fulfillment.

Encouraging Reflection and Self-Awareness

Faith-based education promotes reflection and self-awareness, encouraging students to examine their values, beliefs, and behaviors.

Reflective Practices

Practices such as prayer, meditation, and journaling provide students with opportunities for reflection and introspection. These practices help students develop self-awareness and a deeper understanding of their thoughts, feelings, and motivations.

Ethical Decision-Making

Faith-based education encourages students to consider the ethical implications of their actions and decisions. By reflecting on their values and beliefs, students learn to make choices that align with their moral principles and contribute to their overall personal growth.

Benefits of Faith-Based Education

Academic Success

Studies have shown that students in faith-based schools often perform better academically compared to their peers in non-faith-based schools. The emphasis on discipline, respect, and a strong work ethic contributes to a positive learning environment and academic achievement.

Emotional Well-Being

Faith-based education provides students with emotional and spiritual support, helping them maintain a positive outlook and emotional well-being. The sense of community and belonging in faith-based schools also contributes to lower levels of stress and anxiety among students.

Long-Term Impact

The values and principles instilled through faith-based education have a lasting impact on students, shaping their character and guiding their behavior well into adulthood. The moral foundation, resilience, and sense of purpose developed during their school years continue to influence their personal and professional lives.

Conclusion

Faith plays a crucial role in the holistic development of young individuals. By integrating faith into education, schools help students develop a strong moral foundation, resilience, and a sense of purpose. Faith-based education also encourages reflection and self-awareness, fostering personal growth and ethical decision-making. The benefits of faith-based education extend beyond academic success, contributing to the overall well-being and long-term development of students. Through faith, students are equipped with the values, skills, and support they need to navigate life's challenges and make meaningful contributions to their communities and the world.

**Moral Compass**

One of the most significant benefits of faith-based education is the development of a clear moral compass in students. This moral foundation is integral to guiding their decisions and actions, helping them navigate the complexities of life with integrity and ethical awareness.

Establishing Core Values

Faith-based education instills core values that form the basis of a student's moral compass. These values often include:

1. Honesty: Encouraging students to be truthful in their words and actions.

2. Integrity: Promoting consistency between one's values and behaviors, ensuring actions reflect beliefs.

3. Respect: Teaching students to value and honor the dignity of all individuals, regardless of differences.

4. Compassion: Fostering empathy and a desire to help those in need.

5. Responsibility: Instilling a sense of accountability for one's actions and their impact on others.

These values are woven into the fabric of the educational experience, and reinforced through curriculum, school culture, and daily interactions.

Practical Applications of Core Values

Faith-based education not only teaches core values but also provides practical opportunities for students to apply them. This practical application solidifies these values and helps students understand their importance in real-world contexts.

1. Service Projects: Students engage in community service, applying values like compassion and responsibility by helping those in need.

2. Ethical Discussions: Classrooms become spaces for discussing ethical dilemmas and exploring how core values guide decision-making processes.

3. Role-Playing Activities: Students participate in role-playing scenarios that require them to navigate complex situations using their moral compass.

Influence on Decision-Making

The moral compass developed through faith-based education significantly influences students' decision-making processes. It provides a framework for evaluating choices and actions, ensuring they align with ethical principles and personal values.

1. Ethical Awareness: Students become more aware of the ethical dimensions of their decisions, considering the consequences for themselves and others.

2. Consistency in Behavior: A strong moral foundation promotes consistency in behavior, reducing instances of hypocrisy and fostering trustworthiness.

3. Long-Term Perspective: Students learn to consider the long-term implications of their actions, prioritizing integrity and ethical conduct over short-term gains.

Navigating Life's Complexities

Life is filled with complex situations and difficult decisions. A clear moral compass helps students navigate these challenges with confidence and clarity.

1. Resilience in Adversity: During times of adversity, a strong moral foundation provides stability and guidance, helping students remain true to their values.

2. Conflict Resolution: When faced with conflicts, students use their moral compass to seek fair and respectful solutions, promoting harmony and understanding.

3. Personal Accountability: Students learn to take responsibility for their actions, acknowledging mistakes and striving to make amends.

Conclusion

A key benefit of faith-based education is the development of a clear moral compass in students. This moral foundation, built on core values such as honesty, integrity, respect, compassion, and responsibility, guides their decisions and actions throughout their lives. By providing practical opportunities to apply these values and influencing decision-making processes, faith-based education helps students navigate the complexities of life with integrity and ethical awareness. The result is individuals who are not only academically prepared but also morally grounded, ready to contribute positively to their communities and society at large.

**Emotional Resilience**

Emotional resilience is a vital component of a well-rounded education, and faith-based education plays a significant role in fostering this quality in students. Spiritual practices such as prayer and meditation provide students with tools to manage stress, anxiety, and other emotional challenges. Faith can be a profound source of strength and comfort, particularly during difficult times.

The Role of Spiritual Practices

Spiritual practices are integral to faith-based education, offering students regular opportunities for reflection, connection, and emotional regulation.

1. Prayer: Prayer is a fundamental spiritual practice that allows students to express their thoughts, fears, and hopes. It provides a sense of connection to a higher power, fostering feelings of peace and reassurance. Regular prayer can help students develop a routine that brings stability and calmness to their daily lives.

2. Meditation: Meditation encourages mindfulness and presence, helping students focus on the present moment rather than dwelling on past regrets or future anxieties. Through meditation, students learn to calm their minds, reduce stress, and enhance their emotional well-being.

3. Reflection: Reflective practices, such as journaling or contemplation, allow students to process their experiences and emotions. These practices encourage introspection and self-awareness, helping students understand and manage their feelings more effectively.

Building Emotional Resilience

Faith-based education helps build emotional resilience in several ways:

1. Coping Mechanisms: Spiritual practices provide students with coping mechanisms to handle emotional challenges. Whether through prayer, meditation, or reflection, these practices offer a means of processing and alleviating stress and anxiety.

2. Supportive Community: Faith-based schools often foster a strong sense of community where students feel supported and understood. This network of support is crucial during times of emotional turmoil, providing a sense of belonging and shared strength.

3. Sense of Purpose: Faith offers a sense of purpose and meaning, which can be particularly grounding during difficult times. Understanding that their lives have a higher purpose can help students remain resilient and focused, even when facing adversity.

Managing Stress and Anxiety

Stress and anxiety are common challenges for students, and faith-based education equips them with tools to manage these emotions effectively.

1. Structured Routines: The incorporation of regular spiritual practices into the school day provides a structured routine that helps students feel grounded and less overwhelmed by their academic and personal responsibilities.

2. Mindfulness and Calm: Practices such as meditation promote mindfulness, helping students stay calm and focused. This mindfulness can reduce the impact of stress and anxiety, allowing students to approach their tasks with a clear and composed mindset.

3. Expressive Outlets: Prayer and reflection offer expressive outlets for students to articulate their worries and fears. By verbalizing or writing down their concerns, students can better manage their emotions and reduce their anxiety levels.

Faith as a Source of Strength

Faith itself can be a profound source of strength and comfort, offering students a framework for understanding and overcoming life's challenges.

1. Hope and Optimism: Faith instills hope and optimism, encouraging students to look beyond their immediate difficulties and believe in a positive outcome. This hopeful outlook is essential for maintaining emotional resilience.

2. Trust in a Higher Power: Believing in a higher power provides students with a sense of security and support. Trusting that they are not alone in their struggles can be incredibly comforting and empowering.

3. Moral and Ethical Guidance: Faith offers moral and ethical guidance that can help students navigate challenging situations. Knowing that their actions are aligned with their values provides a sense of confidence and stability.

Practical Examples

1. Stress Relief Workshops: Faith-based schools may offer workshops on stress relief that incorporate spiritual practices such as prayer, meditation, and reflective journaling. These workshops equip students with practical tools to manage their stress.

2. Prayer Groups: Organizing prayer groups where students can come together to pray and support each other creates a sense of community and shared resilience. These groups provide a safe space for students to express their concerns and find collective strength.

3. Meditation Sessions: Regular meditation sessions integrated into the school day can help students develop a routine of mindfulness and emotional regulation. These sessions teach students how to calm their minds and reduce stress effectively.

Conclusion

Emotional resilience is a critical benefit of faith-based education. Spiritual practices such as prayer and meditation provide students with essential tools to manage stress, anxiety, and other emotional challenges. By building coping mechanisms, fostering a supportive community, and offering a sense of purpose and strength, faith-based education helps students develop the emotional resilience needed to navigate life's challenges. This resilience not only enhances their academic performance but also contributes to their overall well-being and personal growth.

## Sense of Purpose

Understanding and embracing one's faith can give students a profound sense of purpose and direction. This sense of purpose helps them set meaningful goals and strive toward a life that aligns with their values and beliefs. Faith-based education plays a crucial role in nurturing this sense of purpose and guiding students in their personal and academic journeys.

Defining Purpose Through Faith

Faith provides a framework for understanding one's place in the world and the larger meaning of life. This understanding is essential for developing a sense of purpose.

1. Spiritual Teachings: Religious teachings often emphasize the importance of leading a purposeful life, guided by principles such as service, compassion, and integrity. These teachings help students identify their personal missions and aspirations.

2. Reflection and Contemplation: Faith-based education encourages regular reflection and contemplation, allowing students to consider their goals, values, and aspirations deeply. This introspective practice helps clarify their sense of purpose.

Setting Meaningful Goals

Faith-based education helps students set meaningful goals that reflect their values and beliefs. This goal-setting process is essential for personal growth and achievement.

1. Aligning with Values: Students are encouraged to set goals that align with their faith and values. This alignment ensures that their pursuits are meaningful and fulfilling, rather than driven by external pressures or superficial desires.

2. Long-Term Vision: Faith-based education fosters a long-term perspective, helping students look beyond immediate rewards to consider their broader impact and legacy. This vision inspires them to set ambitious, yet attainable, goals.

3. Balanced Development: Emphasizing holistic development, faith-based education encourages students to set goals that promote intellectual, emotional, spiritual, and social growth. This balanced approach ensures well-rounded personal development.

Striving Towards a Values-Aligned Life

A strong sense of purpose motivates students to live a life that is consistent with their values and beliefs. Faith-based education supports this endeavor through various means.

1. Ethical Decision-Making: By grounding students in their faith, education helps them make ethical decisions that align with their values. This alignment fosters integrity and authenticity in their actions.

2. Service and Contribution: Many faith-based schools emphasize the importance of service and contribution to others. Students learn that part of living a purposeful life involves helping others and making a positive impact on their communities.

3. Personal Fulfillment: When students pursue goals and activities that resonate with their faith, they experience greater personal fulfillment and satisfaction. This fulfillment reinforces their sense of purpose and motivates them to continue striving towards their ideals.

Practical Applications

Faith-based education integrates practical applications that help students develop and pursue their sense of purpose.

1. Community Service Projects: Engaging in community service projects allows students to apply their faith values in real-world contexts, fostering a sense of contribution and purpose.

2. Mentorship Programs: Mentorship programs connect students with mentors who share their faith and values. These mentors provide guidance and support, helping

students navigate their personal and academic journeys with a clear sense of direction.

3. Goal-Setting Workshops: Workshops on goal-setting and personal development encourage students to articulate their aspirations and create action plans that align with their faith and values.

Long-Term Benefits

The sense of purpose cultivated through faith-based education offers long-term benefits that extend beyond the school years.

1. Career and Life Choices: Students who understand their purpose are better equipped to make informed career and life choices that align with their values. This alignment leads to greater satisfaction and success in their personal and professional lives.

2. Resilience and Perseverance: A clear sense of purpose provides students with the resilience and perseverance needed to overcome challenges and setbacks. They are more likely to stay committed to their goals and continue striving towards their vision.

3. Positive Impact: Students who embrace their purpose are motivated to make a positive impact on their communities and the world. Their actions are driven by a

desire to contribute meaningfully, leading to a legacy of positive change.

Conclusion

A sense of purpose is a significant benefit of faith-based education. By helping students understand and embrace their faith, these educational environments guide them in setting meaningful goals and striving towards a life that aligns with their values and beliefs. The practical applications and long-term benefits of this sense of purpose are profound, leading to personal fulfillment, ethical decision-making, and a lasting positive impact on the world. Faith-based education thus equips students with the direction and motivation they need to lead purposeful and impactful lives.

COMMUNITY AND BELONGING

Community and Belonging in Faith-Based Education

Faith-based education fosters a profound sense of community and belonging. Students who share common beliefs and values often form strong, supportive relationships that significantly enhance their educational experience. This chapter will explore how faith-based schools cultivate a sense of community and the benefits this brings to students' academic and personal development.

Building a Supportive Community

One of the hallmarks of faith-based education is the creation of a supportive community where students feel connected and valued.

1. Shared Beliefs and Values: Common faith and values form the foundation of the school community. This

shared belief system creates a sense of unity and common purpose among students and staff.

2. Inclusive Environment: Faith-based schools strive to create an inclusive environment where all students feel welcomed and accepted. This inclusivity extends to students from different backgrounds, ensuring that everyone feels a sense of belonging.

3. Collaborative Culture: Collaboration and mutual support are emphasized in faith-based schools. Students are encouraged to work together, support one another, and build strong, lasting relationships.

Strengthening Relationships

Faith-based education enhances students' relationships with their peers, teachers, and the broader school community.

1. Peer Relationships: Students often form deep and meaningful friendships based on shared faith and values. These friendships provide emotional support, companionship, and a sense of belonging.

2. Teacher-Student Relationships: Teachers in faith-based schools often serve as mentors and role models. They build strong, supportive relationships with students, fostering trust and mutual respect.

3. Community Engagement: Faith-based schools encourage students to engage with the broader community through service projects, religious activities, and communal events. This engagement strengthens the bonds between students and the community.

Enhancing Educational Experience

A strong sense of community and belonging enhances students' overall educational experience in several ways.

1. Emotional Support: A supportive community provides a network of emotional support for students. This support helps students navigate academic pressures, personal challenges, and social dynamics with greater ease and confidence.

2. Increased Motivation: When students feel connected to their school community, they are more motivated to participate actively in their education. This sense of belonging boosts their engagement and commitment to their studies.

3. Academic Success: Research has shown that students who feel a strong sense of belonging are more likely to succeed academically. The supportive environment of faith-based schools promotes a positive attitude towards learning and academic achievement.

Fostering Personal Growth

Faith-based education not only enhances academic performance but also fosters personal growth and development.

1. Identity Formation: Being part of a faith-based community helps students form a strong sense of identity. They learn to understand and embrace their beliefs and values, which shapes their character and sense of self.

2. Moral Development: The values emphasized in faith-based education, such as compassion, integrity, and respect, contribute to students' moral development. This moral grounding influences their behavior and decision-making.

3. Leadership Skills: Faith-based schools often provide opportunities for students to take on leadership roles within the community. These roles help students develop leadership skills, confidence, and a sense of responsibility.

Activities and Programs Promoting Community

Faith-based schools implement various activities and programs that promote a sense of community and belonging.

1. Religious Services and Gatherings: Regular religious services, prayer meetings, and faith-based gatherings bring students together, reinforcing their shared beliefs and sense of community.

2. Service Projects: Community service projects allow students to work together towards a common goal, fostering teamwork and a sense of purpose.

3. Social Events: Social events such as retreats, picnics, and cultural celebrations provide opportunities for students to connect, build friendships, and strengthen their sense of belonging.

Addressing Challenges

While faith-based schools excel at fostering community, they also face challenges in ensuring inclusivity and respect for diverse perspectives.

1. Balancing Inclusivity and Shared Beliefs: Faith-based schools must balance the promotion of shared beliefs with the need to be inclusive and respectful of different viewpoints. This balance ensures that all students feel valued and included.

2. Addressing Conflicts: Conflicts can arise in any community. Faith-based schools must have strategies in place to address conflicts constructively, promoting understanding and reconciliation.

3. Supporting Diverse Backgrounds: Faith-based schools should strive to support students from diverse backgrounds, ensuring that everyone feels a sense of belonging regardless of their individual differences.

Conclusion

Community and belonging are central to the experience of faith-based education. By fostering a supportive community, strengthening relationships, and enhancing the educational experience, faith-based schools create an environment where students feel connected, valued, and motivated. This sense of belonging not only supports academic success but also promotes personal growth, moral development, and leadership skills. Through various activities and programs, faith-based schools cultivate a vibrant and inclusive community that prepares students to thrive both academically and personally. The benefits of this community extend far beyond the school years, providing a foundation for lifelong connections and a strong sense of identity and purpose.

CHAPTER 04

## GUIDING THE YOUNG

Effective school chaplaincy requires a combination of empathy, active listening, and practical strategies. By understanding the unique needs of young individuals and employing targeted approaches, chaplains can effectively guide students in their faith journey. This chapter will outline key strategies that chaplains can use to support and nurture the spiritual development of students.

Building Trust and Rapport

Active Listening

Active listening is crucial in building trust and rapport with students. Chaplains should:

- Be Present: Give full attention to the student, showing genuine interest in their thoughts and feelings.

- Reflect and Validate: Reflect back what the student has said and validate their emotions, helping them feel heard and understood.

- Avoid Judgment: Create a non-judgmental space where students can openly share their experiences and concerns.

Consistent Presence

Being consistently present and accessible helps students feel comfortable approaching the chaplain. Chaplains should:

- Engage in School Activities: Participate in school events, attend classes, and be visible in common areas.

- Hold Regular Office Hours: Maintain regular office hours where students can drop in for informal conversations or scheduled counseling sessions.

Encouraging Spiritual Practices

Prayer and Meditation

Encouraging regular prayer and meditation practices helps students develop a routine of spiritual reflection. Chaplains can:

- Organize Group Prayer: Hold regular group prayer sessions or meditation circles where students can gather for communal reflection.

- Teach Techniques: Introduce different prayer and meditation techniques, helping students find methods that resonate with them.

Scripture Study

Scripture study deepens students' understanding of their faith and its teachings. Chaplains should:

- Lead Bible Study Groups: Organize and lead Bible study groups where students can explore and discuss scripture.

- Provide Resources: Offer resources such as study guides, commentaries, and access to religious texts.

Facilitating Personal Growth

Service Projects

Involving students in service projects fosters a sense of purpose and compassion. Chaplains can:

- Coordinate Volunteer Opportunities: Arrange volunteer opportunities within the school and the local community.

- Connect Faith and Service: Highlight how service aligns with their faith's teachings on compassion and helping others.

Mentorship Programs

Mentorship programs provide students with guidance and support from older peers or adults. Chaplains should:

- Establish Mentorship Relationships: Pair students with mentors who can provide spiritual and personal guidance.

- Monitor Progress: Regularly check in with both mentors and mentees to ensure the relationship is beneficial and supportive.

Promoting Inclusivity and Respect

Interfaith Activities

Promoting interfaith understanding and respect is crucial in diverse school environments. Chaplains can:

- Organize Interfaith Dialogues: Facilitate discussions that allow students to learn about and appreciate different religious traditions.

- Celebrate Diversity: Organize events that celebrate the religious and cultural diversity within the school.

Conflict Resolution

Chaplains play a key role in mediating conflicts and teaching students how to resolve disagreements respectfully. They should:

- Teach Conflict Resolution Skills: Provide training on active listening, empathy, and finding common ground.

- Mediate Conflicts: Act as neutral mediators in conflicts, helping students navigate disagreements constructively.

Supporting Emotional Well-Being

Counseling and Support

Providing emotional support and counseling is a critical aspect of a chaplain's role. Chaplains should:

- Offer One-on-One Counseling: Provide personalized counseling sessions to support students through personal challenges.

- Create Support Groups: Establish support groups for students dealing with similar issues, such as grief, stress, or family problems.

Promoting Mental Health

Chaplains can promote mental health by integrating spiritual and emotional well-being practices. They can:

- Hold Wellness Workshops: Organize workshops on topics such as stress management, mindfulness, and self-care.

- Encourage Balance: Advocate for a balanced approach to life that includes physical, emotional, and spiritual well-being.

Practical Examples and Case Studies

Example 1: Building Trust Through Consistent Presence

A chaplain at a large urban high school made a point of being visible and accessible to students. By attending school events, visiting classrooms, and being available during lunch breaks, the chaplain built strong relationships with students. This consistent presence made students feel comfortable seeking out the chaplain for support and guidance.

Example 2: Encouraging Spiritual Growth Through Service

At a faith-based school, the chaplain organized a series of community service projects that allowed students to put their faith into action. These projects included volunteering at local shelters, organizing food drives, and participating in environmental clean-up efforts. Through these activities, students developed a deeper understanding of their faith's teachings on compassion and service.

Example 3: Promoting Inclusivity Through Interfaith Dialogues

In a diverse school setting, the chaplain facilitated interfaith dialogues that brought together students from different religious backgrounds. These discussions promoted mutual understanding and respect, helping to create a more inclusive school environment. The chaplain also organized events that celebrated the cultural and religious diversity within the school.

Conclusion

Effective school chaplaincy requires a combination of empathy, active listening, and practical strategies. By building trust and rapport, encouraging spiritual practices, facilitating personal growth, promoting inclusivity and respect, and supporting emotional well-being, chaplains can guide young individuals in their faith journey. Through practical examples and case studies, this chapter has outlined key approaches that chaplains can use to nurture and support the spiritual development of students. By implementing these strategies, chaplains can make a significant positive impact on the lives of young individuals, helping them grow into compassionate, resilient, and ethically grounded individuals.

Building Trust and Rapport

Establishing trust and rapport with students is foundational to effective chaplaincy. This involves demonstrating genuine care and concern for their well-being, and one of the most critical skills in this process is active listening. By truly listening to students' concerns and experiences without judgment, chaplains create a safe space where students feel valued and understood. This section will delve into the importance of active listening and provide practical tips on how chaplains can implement this skill effectively.

Active Listening

Active listening is more than just hearing words; it involves engaging with the speaker and showing genuine interest in their message. For chaplains, active listening is a vital tool in building trust and rapport with students. Here's how to practice active listening effectively:

1. Be Present: Give the student your full attention. This means putting aside distractions, making eye contact, and focusing on the conversation. Presence signals to the student that they are important and that their concerns matter.

2. Show Empathy: Empathy involves understanding and sharing the feelings of another person. When listening to students, chaplains should strive to understand their emotions and perspectives. Reflecting back emotions and showing empathy helps students feel validated and understood.

3. Avoid Judgment: Create a non-judgmental environment where students can express themselves freely. Avoid interrupting or offering unsolicited advice. Instead, listen with an open mind and heart, acknowledging the student's feelings and experiences without passing judgment.

4. Use Reflective Responses: Reflective responses involve paraphrasing or summarizing what the student has said to show that you have understood their message. Phrases like "What I hear you saying is..." or "It sounds like you are feeling..." can be very effective.

5. Ask Open-Ended Questions: Encourage students to share more about their thoughts and feelings by asking open-ended questions. Questions like "Can you tell me more about that?" or "How did that make you feel?" invite deeper conversation and show that you are genuinely interested in their experiences.

6. Provide Non-Verbal Cues: Non-verbal communication, such as nodding, leaning forward, and maintaining eye contact, signals to the student that you are engaged and attentive. These cues reinforce that you are actively listening and present in the moment.

7. Be Patient: Allow students to speak at their own pace without rushing them. Patience demonstrates respect for their process of sharing and can help them feel more comfortable and open.

Creating a Safe Space

Creating a safe space for students to express themselves is crucial in building trust and rapport. A safe space is one where students feel comfortable, respected, and free from judgment. Here are some strategies to create such an environment:

1. Confidentiality: Assure students that their conversations with you are confidential. Understanding that

their privacy will be respected encourages students to speak openly about their concerns.

2. Consistency: Be consistent in your availability and approach. Regularly being present and approachable helps build a reliable foundation where students know they can count on you.

3. Respect Boundaries: Respect the boundaries set by students. Some may not be ready to share deeply personal experiences right away, and that's okay. Building trust takes time, and respecting their pace is essential.

4. Non-Directive Approach: Sometimes, the best way to help is simply to listen without trying to direct the conversation or solve the problem immediately. Allowing students to explore their thoughts and feelings freely can be incredibly therapeutic.

5. Positive Reinforcement: Encourage and affirm students when they share their thoughts and feelings. Positive reinforcement helps build their confidence and reinforces the idea that their voice matters.

Practical Example: Implementing Active Listening

Imagine a scenario where a student approaches the chaplain feeling overwhelmed by academic pressures and personal issues. The chaplain can implement active listening by:

1. Greeting the Student Warmly: Offering a warm and genuine greeting, inviting the student to sit down, and ensuring they feel welcome.

2. Listening Attentively: Putting aside all distractions, maintaining eye contact, and nodding to show understanding as the student shares their concerns.

3. Reflecting and Validating: Saying, "It sounds like you're feeling really stressed about your schoolwork and personal life right now. That must be really tough."

4. Asking Open-Ended Questions: Encouraging further sharing with, "Can you tell me more about what's been going on?"

5. Showing Empathy: Expressing empathy by saying, "I can see why you would feel overwhelmed. It's a lot to handle all at once."

By using these active listening techniques, the chaplain creates a supportive environment where the student feels heard and understood, laying the groundwork for a trusting relationship.

Conclusion

Building trust and rapport with students is essential for effective chaplaincy, and active listening is a critical component of this process. By truly listening to students' concerns and experiences without judgment, chaplains create a safe space where students feel valued and understood. Implementing active listening techniques and creating a supportive environment fosters deeper connections and helps guide students on their faith journey. Through these efforts, chaplains can significantly impact the emotional and spiritual well-being of the young individuals they serve.

Being Present

Being visibly present and accessible within the school is essential for chaplains to build trust and rapport with students. When chaplains actively engage in the school community, they demonstrate their commitment to the well-being of the students and create opportunities for meaningful interactions. This section will explore the importance of presence and practical strategies chaplains can use to integrate themselves into the daily life of the school.

The Importance of Presence

Presence is more than just physical availability; it is about being actively involved and showing genuine interest in the lives of students. Here's why being present is crucial:

1. Building Trust: Regular interaction helps students become familiar with the chaplain, building trust and making it easier for them to seek support when needed.

2. Accessibility: Being present in various settings makes the chaplain more accessible to students, who might be hesitant to seek help in formal settings.

3. Creating Connections: Presence allows chaplains to form deeper connections with students, understanding their needs, concerns, and experiences better.

4. Role Modeling: By being actively involved, chaplains serve as role models, demonstrating commitment, empathy, and engagement.

Practical Strategies for Being Present

1. Attending School Events

- Sports Events: Attend school sports events to support students and celebrate their achievements. Engaging in conversations with students and parents during these events helps build rapport.

- Cultural and Arts Events: Participate in school plays, music concerts, and art exhibitions. Showing interest in students' talents and passions fosters a sense of validation and encouragement.

- Parent-Teacher Meetings: Being present at parent-teacher meetings provides an opportunity to interact with parents and understand the broader context of students' lives.

2. Visiting Classrooms

- Guest Speaking: Offer to speak in classrooms on topics related to faith, ethics, or emotional well-being. This allows students to see the chaplain in a supportive educational role.

- Classroom Visits: Make informal visits to classrooms to observe and interact with students in their learning environment. This visibility shows students that the chaplain is approachable and invested in their education.

3. Engaging During Breaks and Lunchtime

- Lunchtime Conversations: Spend time in the cafeteria or common areas during lunch breaks, engaging in casual conversations with students. This informal setting can make students feel more comfortable opening up.

- Recess Activities: Participate in or observe recess activities, showing interest in students' play and social interactions. This presence helps students see the chaplain as a part of their everyday school life.

4. Hosting Office Hours

- Open Door Policy: Maintain an open-door policy during office hours, encouraging students to drop by for a chat, whether for serious discussions or casual conversations.

- Scheduled Meetings: Offer students the opportunity to schedule one-on-one meetings during these hours for more in-depth support and guidance.

5. Involvement in Extracurricular Activities

- Clubs and Organizations: Participate in or support student clubs and organizations, such as faith-based groups, service clubs, or hobby groups. This involvement shows students that the chaplain values their interests.

- Service Projects: Organize and participate in community service projects, working alongside students and demonstrating the importance of giving back.

Building a Visible and Accessible Presence

To effectively build a visible and accessible presence, chaplains should consider the following:

1. Consistency: Regular and consistent presence is key. Students need to know they can rely on the chaplain being there.

2. Approachability: Maintain a friendly and approachable demeanor. Smile, greet students, and engage in light-hearted conversations.

3. Flexibility: Be flexible in your approach, adapting to the needs and schedules of students. Sometimes, the most meaningful interactions happen spontaneously.

4. Visibility: Make sure students can easily identify and locate you. This might involve having a designated space that is welcoming and accessible.

Practical Example: Implementing Presence

Imagine a scenario where the chaplain decides to be more visible during school hours:

1. Morning Greeting: The chaplain stands at the school entrance in the mornings, greeting students as they arrive. This small gesture starts the day on a positive note and shows students they are valued.

2. Lunchtime Engagement: During lunch breaks, the chaplain sits in the cafeteria, moving from table to table to engage in conversations with different groups of students. These interactions are casual, making it easier for students to share their thoughts and concerns.

3. Event Participation: The chaplain attends a school basketball game, cheering for the students and celebrating their efforts regardless of the outcome. After the game, the chaplain chats with the players, offering encouragement and support.

4. Classroom Visits: The chaplain visits a history class to talk about the ethical implications of historical events, tying in faith perspectives. This educational involvement helps students see the chaplain as a knowledgeable and supportive figure.

Conclusion

Being present is a crucial strategy for chaplains to build trust and rapport with students. By attending school events, visiting classrooms, engaging during breaks and lunchtime, hosting office hours, and participating in extracurricular activities, chaplains can integrate themselves into the daily life of the school. This visible and accessible presence demonstrates a genuine commitment to the well-being of students, fostering deeper connections and creating a supportive environment. Through these efforts, chaplains can significantly impact the spiritual and emotional development of the young individuals they serve.

## Confidentiality

Maintaining confidentiality is a fundamental aspect of the chaplain's role. It ensures that students feel safe sharing their personal and spiritual struggles, knowing that their privacy will be respected. Confidentiality fosters trust, encourages openness, and creates a secure environment where students can seek guidance and support without fear of judgment or exposure. This section will explore the importance of confidentiality and practical strategies for upholding it in all interactions.

The Importance of Confidentiality

Confidentiality is crucial for several reasons:

1. Building Trust: When students know that their conversations with the chaplain are confidential, they are more likely to open up and share their true feelings and concerns.

2. Encouraging Openness: A guarantee of confidentiality encourages students to discuss sensitive issues they might otherwise keep to themselves, facilitating more effective support and guidance.

3. Creating a Safe Space: Confidentiality helps create a safe and secure environment where students feel respected and valued, fostering emotional and spiritual well-being.

Practical Strategies for Maintaining Confidentiality

1. Clearly Communicate Confidentiality Policies

- Initial Conversations: At the beginning of any interaction, clearly explain the confidentiality policy to the student. Ensure they understand that what they share will remain private unless there is a risk of harm to themselves or others.

- Written Policies: Provide written confidentiality policies that outline the boundaries and exceptions. This can be shared during initial meetings or posted in visible areas.

2. Secure Handling of Information

- Private Conversations: Hold conversations in private, secure settings where interruptions and eavesdropping are unlikely.

- Record Keeping: If it is necessary to keep records, ensure they are stored securely and access is restricted. Use encryption and secure storage systems to protect digital records.

3. Training and Awareness

- Ongoing Training: Regularly train staff and volunteers on the importance of confidentiality and how to handle sensitive information appropriately.

- Awareness Campaigns: Promote awareness of the confidentiality policy among students and staff through posters, brochures, and school announcements.

4. Handling Disclosures

- Professional Boundaries: Maintain professional boundaries and ensure that all disclosures are treated with the utmost respect and confidentiality.

- Mandatory Reporting: Be aware of and comply with mandatory reporting laws. If a student discloses information that suggests they are at risk of harm, follow legal and ethical guidelines for reporting while explaining these actions to the student.

5. Consistent Practice

- Regular Reinforcement: Consistently reinforce the importance of confidentiality in all interactions, ensuring that students understand and trust the commitment to their privacy.

- Role Modeling: Demonstrate confidentiality through your own actions, showing students that their privacy is respected and valued.

Practical Example: Implementing Confidentiality

Consider a scenario where a student approaches the chaplain to discuss personal issues:

1. Private Setting: The chaplain invites the student into a private office where the conversation can be held without interruptions.

2. Clear Communication: At the start of the meeting, the chaplain explains the confidentiality policy, reassuring the student that their conversation will remain private unless there is a risk of harm.

3. Active Listening: The chaplain listens attentively to the student's concerns, providing empathetic support and guidance while maintaining a non-judgmental stance.

4. Secure Record Keeping: After the meeting, the chaplain records key points from the conversation in a secure,

confidential system, ensuring that the information is protected and accessible only to authorized personnel.

Balancing Confidentiality and Safety

While confidentiality is paramount, there are situations where it may need to be balanced with the need to ensure safety:

1. Risk of Harm: If a student discloses information that suggests they are at risk of harm or pose a risk to others, the chaplain must take appropriate action to ensure safety. This may involve informing school authorities or contacting external support services.

2. Transparency: When confidentiality must be breached, explain the reasons to the student and involve them in the process as much as possible. This transparency helps maintain trust and respect even in difficult situations.

Conclusion

Maintaining confidentiality is a cornerstone of effective chaplaincy. It builds trust, encourages openness, and creates a safe environment for students to share their personal and spiritual struggles. By clearly communicating confidentiality policies, securely handling information, providing training and awareness, handling disclosures appropriately, and balancing confidentiality with safety, chaplains can uphold this essential principle. Through these efforts, chaplains ensure that students feel valued, respected, and supported, fostering deeper connections and more effective guidance on their faith journeys.

## CHAPTER 05

## ENCOURAGING SPIRITUAL PRACTICES

### Prayer and Meditation

Encouraging students to develop regular prayer or meditation practices is an essential aspect of fostering their spiritual growth. These practices help students build a deeper connection with their faith, manage stress, and find inner peace. This chapter will explore strategies for guiding students in prayer and meditation, providing various methods, and creating opportunities for communal spiritual practices.

The Importance of Prayer and Meditation

Prayer and meditation offer numerous benefits for students, including:

1. Spiritual Connection: These practices deepen students' relationship with their faith and foster a sense of spiritual connection and purpose.

2. Emotional Well-Being: Regular prayer and meditation can reduce stress, and anxiety, and promote overall emotional well-being.

3. Mindfulness and Focus: These practices enhance mindfulness, helping students stay present and focused in their daily lives.

Encouraging Regular Prayer Practices

1. Teaching Different Methods of Prayer

- Personal Prayer: Teach students how to engage in personal prayer, encouraging them to speak openly with their faith about their thoughts, feelings, and needs.

- Structured Prayer: Introduce structured prayers from religious texts or traditions that students can incorporate into their daily routines.

- Creative Prayer: Encourage creative forms of prayer, such as journaling, writing letters to their faith, or using art and music as expressions of prayer.

2. Creating Opportunities for Communal Prayer

- Morning and Evening Prayers: Organize regular communal prayer sessions at the beginning and end of the school day, fostering a sense of community and shared faith.

- Prayer Groups: Establish prayer groups where students can come together to pray, share their experiences, and support one another spiritually.

- Special Prayer Events: Hold special prayer events for significant religious occasions, providing opportunities for students to engage in communal worship and celebration.

3. Providing Resources and Support

- Prayer Guides: Create and distribute prayer guides that offer suggestions and frameworks for personal and communal prayer.

- Prayer Spaces: Designate quiet, private spaces within the school where students can go for personal prayer and reflection.

- Chaplain Support: Offer one-on-one sessions with the chaplain for students seeking guidance on how to develop their prayer practices.

Encouraging Regular Meditation Practices

1. Teaching Different Methods of Meditation

- Mindfulness Meditation: Introduce mindfulness meditation techniques that help students focus on their breath and stay present in the moment.

- Guided Meditation: Provide guided meditations that lead students through calming visualizations and reflections.

- Silent Meditation: Encourage silent meditation practices where students sit quietly and observe their thoughts and feelings without judgment.

2. Creating Opportunities for Communal Meditation

- Meditation Sessions: Organize regular communal meditation sessions, where students can practice mindfulness together in a supportive environment.

- Meditation Retreats: Plan occasional meditation retreats, offering an extended period for deepening their practice and experiencing the benefits of meditation.

- Meditation Clubs: Establish meditation clubs where students can explore different meditation techniques and share their experiences.

3. Providing Resources and Support

- Meditation Guides: Develop and share meditation guides that offer step-by-step instructions for various meditation practices.

- Meditation Spaces: Create designated meditation spaces within the school, equipped with comfortable seating and a peaceful atmosphere.

- Chaplain Support: Offer personalized sessions with the chaplain for students seeking guidance on how to incorporate meditation into their daily lives.

Practical Example: Implementing Prayer and Meditation

Consider a scenario where the chaplain wants to encourage both prayer and meditation among students:

1. Morning Prayer Session: Each morning, the chaplain leads a brief communal prayer session in the school chapel, inviting students and staff to start their day with a moment of spiritual reflection and connection.

2. Mindfulness Meditation Workshop: The chaplain organizes a weekly mindfulness meditation workshop, teaching students techniques for staying present and managing stress. The workshop includes guided meditations and opportunities for students to discuss their experiences.

3. Prayer and Meditation Guides: The chaplain creates comprehensive prayer and meditation guides, and distributes them to students. These guides offer various methods and tips for personal practice, encouraging students to explore and find what works best for them.

4. Designated Spaces: The school designates quiet rooms for prayer and meditation, ensuring students have a peaceful environment to practice. These spaces are available throughout the day, providing flexibility for students to use them as needed.

**Conclusion**

Encouraging students to develop regular prayer or meditation practices is vital for their spiritual and emotional well-being. By teaching different methods of prayer and meditation, creating opportunities for communal practices, and providing resources and support, chaplains can guide students in their spiritual journeys. These practices help students build a deeper connection with their faith, manage stress, and find inner peace, contributing to their overall development and well-being. Through these efforts, chaplains play a crucial role in nurturing the spiritual lives of the young individuals they serve.

Scripture Study

Organizing Bible study groups or faith-based reading sessions is a vital strategy for helping students explore and understand religious texts. These sessions not only deepen students' knowledge of their faith but also encourage them to apply its teachings to their daily lives. This chapter will explore practical approaches to facilitating scripture study, fostering an environment of learning, reflection, and spiritual growth.

The Importance of Scripture Study

Scripture study offers numerous benefits for students, including:

1. Deepening Understanding: Studying religious texts helps students gain a deeper understanding of their faith's teachings, history, and values.

2. Personal Reflection: Engaging with scripture encourages personal reflection and introspection, helping students relate religious teachings to their own lives.

3. Community Building: Group study sessions foster a sense of community and shared purpose, strengthening the bonds between students.

Organizing Bible Study Groups

1. Forming the Groups

- Diverse Participation: Encourage students from different backgrounds and levels of understanding to join, fostering a diverse and inclusive environment.

- Small Groups: Keep the groups small enough to allow for meaningful discussion and personal engagement, ideally between 5-10 participants.

2. Structuring the Sessions

- Regular Meetings: Schedule regular, consistent meeting times to establish a routine and ensure ongoing engagement.

- Thematic Focus: Each session can focus on a specific theme, passage, or book of the Bible, providing structure and direction.

- Guided Discussions: Prepare discussion questions and prompts that encourage critical thinking and personal application of the texts.

3. Facilitating the Discussions

- Active Participation: Encourage all participants to share their thoughts and reflections, creating an open and inclusive dialogue.

- Respectful Environment: Foster a respectful atmosphere where differing viewpoints are welcomed and valued.

- Relevant Applications: Guide students to consider how the teachings of the scripture can be applied to contemporary issues and their own lives.

Faith-Based Reading Sessions

1. Selecting Texts

- Variety of Materials: Choose a range of texts, including different books of the Bible, commentaries, and contemporary faith-based literature.

- Student Input: Involve students in selecting texts that interest them, increasing engagement and relevance.

2. Reading and Reflection

- Assigned Readings: Assign readings before each session, allowing students to come prepared and ready to discuss.

- Reflective Practices: Incorporate reflective practices, such as journaling or group reflection, to help students process and internalize the readings.

3. Interactive Activities

- Creative Projects: Include creative projects, such as art, music, or writing, that allow students to express their understanding of the texts in different ways.

- Role-Playing: Use role-playing activities to help students explore and empathize with different characters and scenarios from the texts.

Providing Resources and Support

1. Study Guides

- Comprehensive Guides: Provide study guides that include summaries, key themes, discussion questions, and reflection prompts.

- Accessible Formats: Ensure that the guides are available in both print and digital formats for easy access.

2. Workshops and Seminars

- Skills Development: Offer workshops and seminars on effective study techniques, critical thinking, and theological interpretation.

- Guest Speakers: Invite guest speakers, such as religious scholars or community leaders, to provide additional insights and perspectives.

3. One-on-One Support

- Personal Guidance: Offer one-on-one sessions with the chaplain for students seeking deeper understanding or personalized guidance in their scripture study.

- Mentorship Programs: Pair students with mentors who can support and guide them in their faith journey.

Practical Example: Implementing Scripture Study

Imagine a scenario where the chaplain organizes a Bible study group for interested students:

1. Initial Meeting: The chaplain holds an initial meeting to introduce the group, explain the purpose, and discuss the structure and expectations. Students are invited to share their interests and preferences for topics.

2. Regular Sessions: The group meets weekly in a comfortable, quiet space conducive to discussion and reflection. Each session begins with a prayer or meditation to center the participants.

3. Thematic Focus: For one month, the group focuses on the Book of Psalms, exploring themes of praise, lament, and thanksgiving. The chaplain provides a study guide with key passages, questions, and reflection prompts.

4. Active Participation: During the sessions, the chaplain encourages each student to share their thoughts and

experiences related to the readings. Discussions are guided to ensure everyone has the opportunity to contribute.

5. Creative Projects: To deepen their engagement, students are invited to create a piece of art or write a poem inspired by a Psalm. These projects are shared and discussed in a subsequent session.

**Conclusion**

Organizing Bible study groups and faith-based reading sessions is a powerful way to help students explore and understand religious texts. By structuring sessions thoughtfully, facilitating engaging discussions, and providing a variety of resources and support, chaplains can foster a deeper connection to faith and encourage students to apply these teachings to their lives. Through these practices, students gain not only knowledge but also spiritual growth, personal reflection, and a sense of community, enriching their overall educational experience.

**Service Projects**

Involving students in community service projects that align with their faith values is a powerful way to strengthen their faith and teach the importance of compassion and service to others. These projects provide practical opportunities for students to live out their beliefs, fostering a deeper understanding of their faith and its application in the world. This chapter will explore strategies for organizing and implementing effective service projects that engage students and enhance their spiritual and moral development.

The Importance of Service Projects

Service projects offer numerous benefits for students, including:

1. Faith in Action: Students learn to apply their faith values in real-world settings, experiencing firsthand the impact of their beliefs on their actions and community.

2. Compassion and Empathy: Engaging in service fosters a sense of compassion and empathy, helping students understand and respond to the needs of others.

3. Community Engagement: Service projects connect students to their community, promoting a sense of belonging and social responsibility.

4. Personal Growth: Through service, students develop important life skills, such as teamwork, leadership, and problem-solving, contributing to their overall personal growth.

Organizing Service Projects

1. Identifying Needs

- Community Assessment: Conduct an assessment of the local community to identify areas of need where students can make a meaningful impact. This might include food insecurity, environmental issues, or support for marginalized groups.

- Student Input: Involve students in the process of identifying service opportunities. This engagement increases their investment and ensures that projects resonate with their interests and values.

2. Aligning with Faith Values

- Faith-Based Themes: Choose projects that reflect the core values and teachings of the students' faith, such as compassion, justice, and stewardship. For example, organizing a food drive can reflect teachings on feeding the hungry, while an environmental clean-up aligns with stewardship of the earth.

- Educational Component: Incorporate discussions and reflections on how the service projects connect to faith teachings. This helps students understand the spiritual significance of their actions.

3. Planning and Coordination

- Detailed Planning: Develop a detailed plan for each service project, including objectives, tasks, timelines, and resources needed. Clear planning ensures that projects are well-organized and effective.

- Collaboration: Collaborate with local organizations, charities, and community leaders to maximize the impact of the service projects and provide students with diverse experiences.

Implementing Service Projects

1. Engaging Students

- Inclusive Participation: Ensure that all students have the opportunity to participate, regardless of their background or abilities. Inclusive participation fosters a sense of community and shared purpose.

- Roles and Responsibilities: Assign specific roles and responsibilities to students, encouraging leadership and accountability. This might include project coordination, communication, and logistics.

2. Providing Support and Guidance

- Supervision and Mentorship: Provide supervision and mentorship throughout the project. Chaplains and other adult leaders should offer guidance, support, and encouragement, helping students navigate challenges and reflect on their experiences.

- Skill Development: Offer training and skill development as needed, such as first aid, environmental awareness, or effective communication. These skills enhance the students' ability to contribute effectively.

3. Reflection and Evaluation

- Post-Project Reflection: After each project, hold reflection sessions where students can share their experiences, discuss what they learned, and explore the impact of their actions. Reflection deepens the spiritual and emotional significance of the service.

- Evaluation and Feedback: Evaluate the success of the project and gather feedback from students and community partners. Use this feedback to improve future projects and ensure they continue to meet the needs of the community and align with faith values.

Practical Example: Implementing a Service Project

Imagine a scenario where the chaplain organizes a community garden project:

1. Identifying the Need: After conducting a community assessment, the chaplain identifies a need for fresh produce in a local food desert. The community garden project aligns with the faith value of feeding the hungry.

2. Planning: The chaplain and a group of students develop a detailed plan, including selecting a location, gathering resources, and setting a timeline. They collaborate with a local gardening organization for expertise and support.

3. Engagement: Students are divided into teams, each responsible for different aspects of the project, such as

planting, maintenance, and community outreach. Roles are assigned based on interests and skills.

4. Implementation: Under the guidance of the chaplain and gardening experts, students prepare the soil, plant seeds, and tend to the garden. Regular check-ins and support ensure the project runs smoothly.

5. Reflection: After the first harvest, a reflection session is held where students share their experiences and discuss the project's impact on the community and their understanding of faith. The project is evaluated, and feedback is gathered for future improvements.

Conclusion

Involving students in community service projects that align with their faith values is a powerful way to strengthen their faith and teach the importance of compassion and service to others. By identifying community needs, planning and coordinating projects, engaging students, providing support, and facilitating reflection, chaplains can create meaningful service opportunities that enhance students' spiritual and personal growth. These projects not only benefit the community but also help students develop important life skills and a deeper understanding of their faith in action. Through these efforts, chaplains play a crucial role in nurturing compassionate, responsible, and spiritually grounded individuals.

CHAPTER 06

---

# PROMOTING INCLUSIVITY AND RESPECT

### Interfaith Activities

In today's diverse educational environments, promoting inclusivity and respect is essential. One effective way to achieve this is through organizing interfaith activities. These events and discussions can foster understanding, respect, and appreciation for different religious traditions among students. This chapter will explore strategies for creating meaningful interfaith activities that encourage students to learn about and celebrate religious diversity.

The Importance of Interfaith Activities

Interfaith activities offer numerous benefits for students, including:

1. Understanding and Respect: These activities help students understand and respect different religious beliefs and practices, reducing prejudice and promoting tolerance.

2. Cultural Competence: Exposure to diverse religious traditions enhances students' cultural competence, preparing them to thrive in a multicultural world.

3. Community Building: Interfaith activities foster a sense of community and solidarity, bringing students together through shared learning and dialogue.

Organizing Interfaith Events

1. Planning and Preparation

- Identify Objectives: Clearly define the goals of the interfaith activities, such as promoting understanding, fostering dialogue, or celebrating diversity.

- Engage Stakeholders: Involve students, staff, religious leaders, and community members in the planning process to ensure diverse perspectives and support.

- Choose Inclusive Themes: Select themes that are relevant and inclusive, such as common values, peace, compassion, and social justice.

2. Types of Interfaith Events

- Panel Discussions: Organize panel discussions featuring representatives from different religious traditions.

These panels can address topics such as faith in daily life, ethical issues, or interfaith cooperation.

- Cultural Celebrations: Host cultural celebrations that highlight the traditions, music, food, and rituals of various religions. These events provide a festive and engaging way to learn about different faiths.

- Interfaith Dialogues: Facilitate small group dialogues where students can share their religious experiences and ask questions in a respectful and supportive environment.

- Workshops and Seminars: Conduct workshops and seminars on topics such as religious literacy, interfaith conflict resolution, and the role of faith in social issues.

3. Creating Inclusive Spaces

- Safe and Respectful Environment: Ensure that all interfaith activities are conducted in a safe and respectful environment where students feel comfortable sharing and learning.

- Ground Rules: Establish ground rules for discussions, such as listening without interrupting, respecting different viewpoints, and avoiding proselytizing.

Encouraging Student Participation

1. Inclusive Invitations

- Broad Outreach: Use various channels to invite students to participate, ensuring that all religious groups within the school are represented.

- Personal Invitations: Personally invite students from different religious backgrounds to ensure they feel welcomed and valued.

2. Active Engagement

- Interactive Activities: Incorporate interactive activities, such as group discussions, role-playing, and collaborative projects, to keep students engaged and involved.

- Student Leadership: Encourage students to take leadership roles in organizing and facilitating interfaith activities, empowering them to become advocates for inclusivity.

Providing Resources and Support

1. Educational Materials

- Resource Packs: Provide resource packs that include information on various religious traditions, key beliefs, practices, and important holidays.

- Reading Lists: Offer reading lists with books, articles, and online resources on interfaith dialogue and religious literacy.

2. Facilitation Training

- Workshops for Facilitators: Conduct workshops to train students and staff in effective facilitation techniques, ensuring that interfaith activities are well-managed and inclusive.

- Conflict Resolution Skills: Teach conflict resolution skills to help facilitators manage any disagreements or misunderstandings that may arise during discussions.

3. Ongoing Support

- Chaplain Involvement: Ensure that chaplains are actively involved in interfaith activities, providing guidance, support, and mentorship to students.

- Community Partnerships: Build partnerships with local religious organizations and interfaith groups to enhance the resources and support available for interfaith activities.

Practical Example: Implementing Interfaith Activities

Imagine a scenario where the chaplain organizes an interfaith week at the school:

1. Panel Discussion: The week begins with a panel discussion featuring representatives from Christianity, Islam, Judaism, Hinduism, and Buddhism. Each panelist shares insights into their faith and how it guides their daily lives.

2. Cultural Celebration: The school hosts a cultural celebration where students can sample foods, listen to music,

and observe traditional dances and rituals from various religious traditions.

3. Interfaith Dialogue Circles: Small interfaith dialogue circles are formed, allowing students to share their own religious experiences and ask questions about other faiths. These circles are facilitated by trained students and staff.

4. Workshops: Workshops on topics such as religious literacy and conflict resolution are held, providing students with deeper insights and practical skills for engaging in interfaith dialogue.

5. Reflection and Feedback: At the end of the week, a reflection session is held where students can share their experiences and provide feedback. This session helps the chaplain and organizers understand the impact of the activities and plan future events.

Conclusion

Promoting inclusivity and respect through interfaith activities is essential in today's diverse educational environments. By organizing events and discussions that encourage students to learn about and appreciate different religious traditions, chaplains can foster understanding, respect, and community. Through careful planning, inclusive invitations, active engagement, and ongoing support, these activities can significantly enhance students' cultural competence and prepare them for a multicultural world. Interfaith activities not only benefit the students but also contribute to a more inclusive and harmonious school environment, where diversity is celebrated and valued.

## Conflict Resolution

Conflicts arising from religious or cultural differences can present significant challenges in diverse educational settings. As a chaplain, mediating these conflicts and teaching students conflict resolution skills based on mutual respect and understanding is crucial. This chapter will explore strategies for effectively mediating conflicts and equipping students with the skills needed to navigate and resolve disagreements constructively.

The Importance of Conflict Resolution

Effective conflict resolution is essential for several reasons:

1. Promoting Harmony: Resolving conflicts peacefully fosters a harmonious school environment where all students feel safe and respected.

2. Enhancing Understanding: Conflict resolution provides opportunities for students to understand different perspectives and learn from one another.

3. Building Skills: Teaching conflict resolution equips students with valuable life skills that they can use in various

aspects of their lives, promoting personal growth and social responsibility.

Mediation Strategies for Chaplains

1. Creating a Safe Space

- Neutral Ground: Ensure that conflicts are addressed in a neutral, safe space where all parties feel comfortable and respected.

- Ground Rules: Establish ground rules for mediation sessions, such as listening without interrupting, respecting each other's viewpoints, and maintaining confidentiality.

2. Active Listening and Empathy

- Listen Actively: Listen to each party's perspective without judgment, demonstrating genuine interest and concern for their feelings and experiences.

- Show Empathy: Acknowledge and validate each party's emotions, helping them feel heard and understood.

3. Identifying Common Ground

- Shared Values: Focus on identifying shared values and common goals that can serve as a foundation for resolving the conflict.

- Mutual Interests: Encourage parties to express their interests and needs, looking for areas of overlap and mutual benefit.

4. Facilitating Constructive Dialogue

- Open Communication: Encourage open and honest communication, helping parties express their feelings and viewpoints clearly and respectfully.

- Reframe Negative Statements: Help parties reframe negative or accusatory statements into more constructive and positive language.

5. Developing Solutions

- Brainstorming: Facilitate a brainstorming session where parties can suggest potential solutions, emphasizing collaboration and creativity.

- Evaluating Options: Guide the parties in evaluating the proposed solutions, considering their feasibility and fairness.

6. Agreement and Follow-Up

- Reaching Agreement: Help parties reach a mutually acceptable agreement that addresses the core issues and meets their needs.

- Follow-Up: Schedule follow-up sessions to monitor progress and ensure that the agreement is being upheld and remains effective.

Teaching Conflict Resolution Skills

1. Educational Workshops

- Conflict Resolution Training: Conduct workshops that teach students essential conflict resolution skills, such as active listening, empathy, and negotiation.

- Role-Playing: Use role-playing exercises to help students practice and apply their conflict resolution skills in simulated scenarios.

2. Incorporating Conflict Resolution into Curriculum

- Classroom Discussions: Integrate discussions on conflict resolution into relevant subjects, such as social studies or ethics, providing a theoretical framework and practical examples.

- Collaborative Projects: Encourage collaborative projects that require students to work together, fostering teamwork and conflict resolution in real-world contexts.

3. Peer Mediation Programs

- Training Peer Mediators: Establish a peer mediation program where selected students are trained to mediate conflicts among their peers.

- Support and Supervision: Provide ongoing support and supervision for peer mediators, ensuring they have the resources and guidance needed to be effective.

4. Promoting a Culture of Respect

- Respectful Communication: Encourage respectful communication throughout the school, promoting an environment where differences are acknowledged and valued.

- Celebrating Diversity: Organize events and activities that celebrate cultural and religious diversity, fostering a sense of inclusivity and mutual respect.

Practical Example: Implementing Conflict Resolution

Consider a scenario where a conflict arises between students of different religious backgrounds:

1. Initial Mediation Session: The chaplain arranges a mediation session in a private, neutral space. Ground rules are established, and each student is given the opportunity to share their perspective while the chaplain listens actively and empathetically.

2. Identifying Common Ground: The chaplain helps the students identify shared values, such as respect, tolerance, and the importance of community. This common ground serves as a foundation for resolving the conflict.

3. Constructive Dialogue: Through guided dialogue, the chaplain encourages the students to express their feelings and viewpoints constructively. Negative statements are reframed into positive language.

4. Developing Solutions: The students brainstorm potential solutions, such as organizing an interfaith dialogue

event to promote understanding and respect. The chaplain guides them in evaluating and selecting the best solution.

5. Agreement and Follow-Up: An agreement is reached, and the chaplain schedules follow-up sessions to ensure the agreement is upheld and the relationship between the students continues to improve.

Conclusion

Mediating conflicts arising from religious or cultural differences and teaching students conflict resolution skills based on mutual respect and understanding are essential components of promoting inclusivity and respect in schools. By creating a safe space, actively listening, identifying common ground, facilitating constructive dialogue, developing solutions, and providing ongoing support, chaplains can effectively mediate conflicts and equip students with the skills needed to navigate disagreements constructively. Through these efforts, chaplains foster a harmonious and inclusive school environment where diversity is celebrated and respected.

Inclusive Practices

Ensuring that all school activities and programs are inclusive and respectful of diverse religious beliefs is essential in fostering an environment of mutual respect and understanding. As a chaplain, advocating for policies that support religious freedom and expression is a crucial part of this effort. This chapter will explore strategies for implementing inclusive practices and advocating for policies that respect and celebrate religious diversity.

The Importance of Inclusive Practices

Inclusive practices are vital for several reasons:

1. Promoting Equality: Ensuring inclusivity in school activities and programs promotes equality and respect for all students, regardless of their religious beliefs.

2. Enhancing Community: Inclusive practices help build a cohesive and supportive school community where diversity is celebrated.

3. Supporting Well-Being: When students feel respected and included, their emotional and psychological well-being is enhanced, leading to a more positive educational experience.

Implementing Inclusive Practices

1. Inclusive Curriculum

   - Diverse Perspectives: Integrate diverse religious perspectives into the curriculum, ensuring that students learn about various religious traditions and their contributions to history, culture, and society.

- Inclusive Materials: Use teaching materials that reflect the religious diversity of the student body, promoting a balanced and respectful representation of different faiths.

2. Inclusive Events and Celebrations

- Multifaith Celebrations: Organize events and celebrations that acknowledge and respect the various religious holidays and traditions represented in the school community.

- Shared Values: Focus on shared values and universal themes, such as compassion, justice, and community, when planning school-wide events.

3. Inclusive Policies and Procedures

- Dress Codes: Ensure that dress codes respect religious attire and symbols, allowing students to express their faith through their clothing and accessories.

- Dietary Needs: Provide meal options that accommodate religious dietary restrictions in the school cafeteria, ensuring that all students have access to food that aligns with their beliefs.

- Religious Observances: Respect religious observances by allowing excused absences for religious holidays and accommodating prayer times and spaces within the school.

4. Creating Safe and Respectful Spaces

- Interfaith Rooms: Designate interfaith rooms or quiet spaces where students can pray, meditate, or reflect, respecting their need for spiritual practices during the school day.

- Safe Zones: Establish safe zones where students can discuss their religious beliefs and experiences without fear of judgment or discrimination.

5. Training and Professional Development

- Staff Training: Provide regular training for teachers and staff on religious diversity, cultural competence, and inclusive practices, ensuring they are equipped to support a diverse student body.

- Professional Development: Encourage continuous professional development on topics related to inclusivity and respect, fostering an environment of ongoing learning and improvement.

Advocating for Inclusive Policies

1. Policy Development

- Inclusive Policies: Advocate for the development of school policies that explicitly support religious freedom and expression, ensuring that all students' rights are protected.

- Consultation: Involve students, parents, and community leaders in the policy development process, ensuring that diverse perspectives are considered and respected.

2. Implementation and Enforcement

- Clear Communication: Clearly communicate the school's inclusive policies to students, staff, and parents, ensuring everyone understands their rights and responsibilities.

- Consistent Enforcement: Ensure that policies are consistently enforced, addressing any violations promptly and fairly to maintain an inclusive environment.

3. Support and Resources

- Resource Allocation: Allocate resources to support the implementation of inclusive practices, such as funding for interfaith events, training programs, and inclusive materials.

- Support Networks: Establish support networks for students from diverse religious backgrounds, providing them with additional resources and guidance.

Practical Example: Implementing Inclusive Practices

Imagine a scenario where the chaplain works to implement inclusive practices in a diverse school:

1. Inclusive Curriculum: The chaplain collaborates with teachers to integrate lessons on various religious traditions into the social studies curriculum, ensuring students learn about different faiths and their cultural significance.

2. Multifaith Celebrations: The school organizes a multifaith celebration week, featuring events that highlight different religious holidays, traditions, and values. Activities include cultural performances, food fairs, and discussion panels.

3. Inclusive Policies: The chaplain advocates for policies that respect religious attire and dietary needs, ensuring that students can wear religious symbols and have access to appropriate meal options in the cafeteria.

4. Safe and Respectful Spaces: An interfaith room is designated within the school where students can pray or meditate. The chaplain also establishes safe zones for open discussions about religious beliefs.

5. Staff Training: Regular training sessions are held for teachers and staff on religious diversity and inclusive practices. The chaplain invites guest speakers from different faith communities to provide insights and share experiences.

Conclusion

Implementing inclusive practices and advocating for policies that support religious freedom and expression are essential steps in promoting inclusivity and respect in schools. By developing an inclusive curriculum, organizing multifaith events, creating safe spaces, providing training, and enforcing supportive policies, chaplains can foster an environment where all students feel respected and valued. These efforts contribute to a cohesive and supportive school community that celebrates diversity and promotes equality. Through these inclusive practices, chaplains play a crucial role in ensuring that the school environment is welcoming and respectful for students of all religious backgrounds.

# CONCLUSION

The role of a school chaplain is integral to the spiritual and moral development of students. By providing spiritual guidance, pastoral care, and promoting inclusivity, chaplains play a crucial role in shaping the character and faith of young individuals. Through their dedicated efforts, chaplains help create a nurturing and supportive educational environment where students can thrive both academically and spiritually.

Spiritual Guidance

Chaplains offer students the opportunity to explore and deepen their faith through prayer, meditation, and scripture study. These practices not only foster a strong spiritual foundation but also promote emotional well-being and resilience. By encouraging regular spiritual practices, chaplains help students connect with their faith in meaningful ways, guiding them on their personal journeys.

Pastoral Care

Pastoral care is a cornerstone of the chaplain's role, providing essential emotional and spiritual support to students. Through active listening, empathy, and confidential counseling, chaplains offer a safe space for students to share their struggles and seek guidance. This support helps students navigate the challenges of adolescence, fostering personal growth and emotional resilience.

Promoting Inclusivity

Chaplains are pivotal in promoting inclusivity and respect within the school community. By organizing interfaith activities, mediating conflicts, and advocating for inclusive policies, chaplains ensure that all students feel valued and respected, regardless of their religious or cultural backgrounds. These efforts create a harmonious and supportive environment where diversity is celebrated and every student feels a sense of belonging.

Service Projects

Involving students in service projects that align with their faith values teaches the importance of compassion and service to others. These projects provide practical opportunities for students to live out their beliefs, fostering a deeper understanding of their faith and its application in the world. Through service, students develop a sense of responsibility, empathy, and community engagement.

Building Trust and Rapport

By being visibly present and accessible within the school, chaplains build trust and rapport with students. This consistent presence makes chaplains approachable and reinforces their commitment to the well-being of the school community. Through these relationships, chaplains become trusted mentors and role models, guiding students in their spiritual and moral development.

Conclusion

In summary, the role of a school chaplain is multifaceted and essential in fostering the spiritual and moral development of students. Through spiritual guidance, pastoral care, promoting inclusivity, and engaging students in service, chaplains create a nurturing and supportive educational environment. Their dedicated efforts help shape the character and faith of young individuals, preparing them to thrive both academically and spiritually. By embracing this vital role, chaplains contribute to a positive and inclusive school culture that celebrates diversity and fosters a sense of community and belonging.

www.ingramcontent.com/pod-product-compliance
Lightning Source LLC
Chambersburg PA
CBHW071330130726

47996CB00002B/694